OPOSSUMS

NIGHTTIME ANIMALS

Lynn M. Stone

The Rourke Corporation, Inc.
Vero Beach, Florida 32964

Edited by Sandra A. Robinson

PHOTO CREDITS
© Lynn M. Stone: cover, title page, pages 4, 7, 10, 13, 21; © Breck
Kent: pages 8, 12, 15, 18; © Tom Ulrich: page 17

Library of Congress Cataloging-in-Publication Data

Stone, Lynn M.
  Opossums / by Lynn M. Stone.
    p. cm. — (Nighttime animals)
  Summary: Discusses the habitats, physical characteristics, and
habits of the opossum.
  ISBN 0-86593-295-6
  1. Opossums—Juvenile literature. [1. Opossums.]
I. Title. II. Series: Stone, Lynn M. Nighttime animals.
QL737.M34S78 1993
599.2—dc20   93-10724
                                                           CIP
                                                            AC

TABLE OF CONTENTS

OPOSSUMS

Pretending to be asleep is called "playing possum." It's a trick someone learned from the "possum" itself long ago.

The North American "possum" is really the Virginia opossum. The word "possum" describes a group of animals in and around Australia.

Like the Australian possums, however, America's opossum is a **marsupial.** Marsupials are mammals that keep their youngsters in a body pouch. The kangaroo is a marsupial. The night-loving opossum is the only marsupial in North America.

The night-loving Virginia opossum is
North America's only marsupial

WHERE OPOSSUMS LIVE

The Virginia opossum lives throughout the eastern half of the United States, north into southeastern Canada and south into Mexico and Costa Rica. Virginia opossums also live along the Pacific coast, from California north to British Columbia. The opossum was not found in the West until 1890, when someone released captive opossums.

The opossum's favorite **habitat,** or home area, is forest or brush near a stream or swamp. Opossums also live around farmland and in the wooded parts of many cities.

The favorite habitat of the opossum is woodland

HOW OPOSSUMS LOOK

Opossums have a coat of underfur beneath long, shaggy guard hairs. Opossums are usually grayish white. They have a long, rather pointed pink nose and a ratlike tail. The opossum sometimes loses part of its nearly hairless tail from frostbite.

Opossums have a thumblike toe on each hind foot. That clawless toe moves easily and helps the short-legged opossum grasp branches.

Opossums weigh 4 to 15 pounds.

The unusual hind foot of an opossum has four clawed toes and a clawless, thumblike toe

WHAT OPOSSUMS EAT

Opossums are common partly because they have no trouble finding food. The opossum doesn't see well, but it has a keen sense of smell. Opossums are **omnivorous.** They will eat almost anything—fruit, vegetables, eggs, garbage, beetles, ants, worms and even rattlesnakes. Now and then, an opossum raids a chicken coop.

The opossum is **prey,** or food, for **predators** such as bobcats, coyotes and great horned owls.

Because they feed on road-killed animals, opossums themselves are often struck by cars.

A night hunter, the great horned owl sometimes snags an opossum

The mountain possum of Australia is a marsupial relative of America's opossum

Even at an early age, opossums are acrobats

PLAYING POSSUM

When an opossum "plays possum," it pretends to be dead. It lies flat on the ground. The opossum usually opens its mouth and does not move when it is poked.

Many predators are excited by motion. An opossum that fakes death may trick a predator into not attacking.

Scientists don't know if an opossum really chooses to "play possum," or if the opossum faints. "Playing possum" may last for a minute, or for an hour or more.

Rather than "playing possum," an opossum's best defense may be sharp teeth and a handy hollow log

OPOSSUM HABITS

Opossums are **nocturnal**—creatures of the night. An opossum may wander two miles on its night prowl. Along the way, it may climb, dig and even swim as it searches for food.

The opossum usually lives alone. When it is cold, however, four or five may den up together in a hollow tree. When they are not together, opossums probably give each other messages by using body scents.

*Adult opossums don't generall'
seek each other's company,
except during courtship*

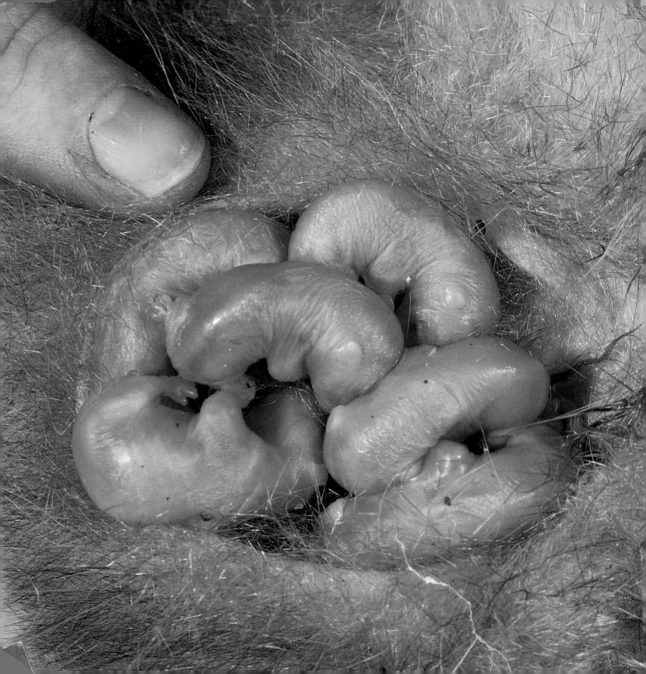

BABY OPOSSUMS

Most mother opossums raise two **litters** each year. Each litter often has 20 or more tiny babies. All 20 could fit in a tablespoon!

Like other newborn marsupial babies, opossums look nothing like their parents. They have no fur, and their hind legs are almost useless.

After birth, newborn opossums crawl into their mother's pouch. They stay there for several weeks, living on mother's milk.

Tiny baby opossums, shown here in their mother's pouch, are born long before they are fully developed

OPOSSUMS GROWING UP

A mother opossum can feed only 13 babies in her pouch. Several of her babies die soon after birth for lack of food.

The babies that live begin to leave the pouch when they are 10 weeks old. At that time they often ride on their mother's back.

Opossums grow up very quickly. They are adults by the time they are three or four months old. Almost all of them live no more than two years.

With mother nearby, a young opossum explores a tree limb

OPOSSUMS AND PEOPLE

Opossums are among the few wild mammals that seem to be right at home near people and their buildings. Opossums live over a much wider area of North America now than they did in 1620 when the English settlers reached Massachusetts.

Sometimes people hunt opossums for food and fur. Opossum fur, however, does not bring high prices.

Glossary

habitat (HAB uh tat) — the kind of place in which an animal lives, such as a forest

hibernate (HI ber nate) — to enter the sleeplike state in which certain animals survive winter

litter (LIH ter) — a group of babies born together of the same mother

marsupial (mar SOOP ee ul) — a family of mammals; the females have a pouch for raising the young, which are born not fully formed

nocturnal (nahk TURN nul) — active at night

omnivorous (ahm NIHV or us) — eating both plants and animals

predator (PRED uh tor) — an animal that kills other animals for food

prey (PRAY) — an animal that is hunted for food by another animal

INDEX